Be Streetwise

**Towns are exciting places to explore, but they can be dangerous.
All detectives need to be properly briefed and equipped.**

Always tell an adult where you are going, how you are getting there, and when you expect to be back.

Wear a watch so you don't need to ask what the time is. Check opening times. Always let a parent know if you are delayed.

Take enough money for your return fare, and both change and a Phonecard for phone calls.

Don't talk to strangers. Before you go out, talk to an adult about who to ask for help in an emergency. (These may include police officers, traffic wardens, bus drivers, and post office, bank or station staff).

Keep your hand or foot against your belongings.

If you have a bicycle, learn how to use it safely.

Never play on building sites, on roads or on other people's property.

Try not to go out alone, and be home before dark.

Learn how to use a public phone, and how to make reverse charge and 999 calls.

Have an up-to-date map, and check transport timetables.

Never accept lifts or invitations into private buildings, even if you are very tired or lost.

Know the Green Cross Code. Read the Highway Code.

Always look where you are going. Don't walk along looking up at buildings, or step backwards into the road.

Never drop litter. Look for a bin or take it home with you.

Above all, use your common sense.

First published in 1990 by
YOUNG LIBRARY LTD
3 The Old Brushworks
56 Pickwick Road
Corsham, Wiltshire SN13 9BX

© Copyright 1990 Jane Launchbury and Selma Montford
All rights reserved

ISBN 1 85429 000 2

Printed and bound in Hong Kong

Contents

The Detective's Home

What place do you know best in the world? Of course, your own home. But how well do you really know it?

Could you describe your home to strangers over the telephone, so that they would recognise it? What makes your home different from the one next door?

Detectives need to know how to look for clues, and report their findings accurately. So begin by having a good look at the outside of your home.

Homes come in all shapes and sizes, and have different terms to describe them. Have a look at the picture below, and decide what sort of building your home is in.

Then go outside and look up at the roof of your home. Perhaps you can't see it because it is flat. If it slopes, is it made of tiles, slates, or thatch? Does it have dormer windows? Are there any chimneys?

What is your home made of? The outside walls may be brick or stone, or covered by wooden weather boarding, tiles, or slate. It may be clad with stone or pebbledash, or have a smooth coat of painted plaster. Modern buildings might be made of concrete slabs, or even of metal or glass.

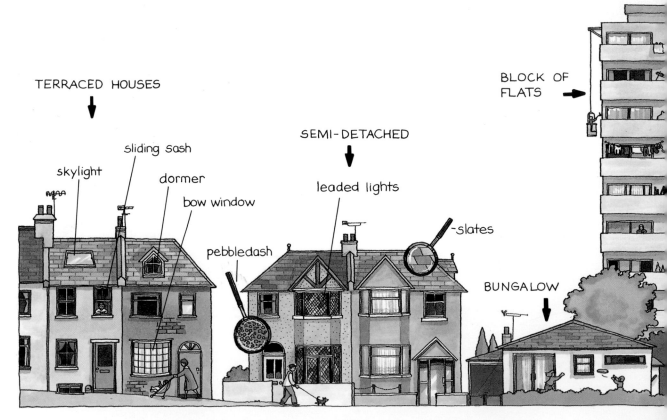

The two main types of window are sash, which are raised and lowered on pulleys, and casement, which swing open on hinges like doors. There are also fixed panes, which are not intended to open. You can also find louvred windows, stained glass, and many other varieties.

Have a look at your own windows. Then look at the windows in the picture, and see if you can identify the types in your home.

How about doors? How many are there on the outside of your home? Is the main door at the front? What colour is it? Is there a porch?

If there is a garden, yard, balcony, or open space around your home, could you describe this too? Things like garages, sheds, and big trees are all useful identifying features.

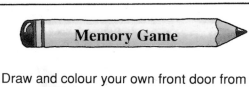

Memory Game

Draw and colour your own front door from memory. Make sure you remember to put in the letterbox, number, bell, keyhole etc.

Now compare it with the real thing!

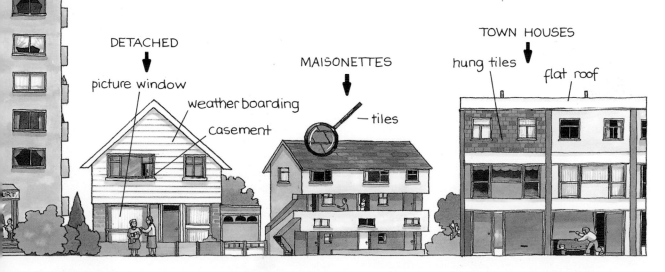

DETACHED

picture window

weather boarding

casement

MAISONETTES

— tiles

TOWN HOUSES

hung tiles

flat roof

The Detective's Den

Which room do you spend one third of your life in? Clue: for most of the time you have your eyes shut. That's right, it's the bedroom.

But how well do you really know your own bedroom? Could you find your way around it in the dark, without tripping over furniture?

Do you remember which way the window opens? Would you be able to avoid the squeaky floorboard?

A good way of getting to know your room better, is to make a simple diagram of it. This is called a plan.

Making a Plan

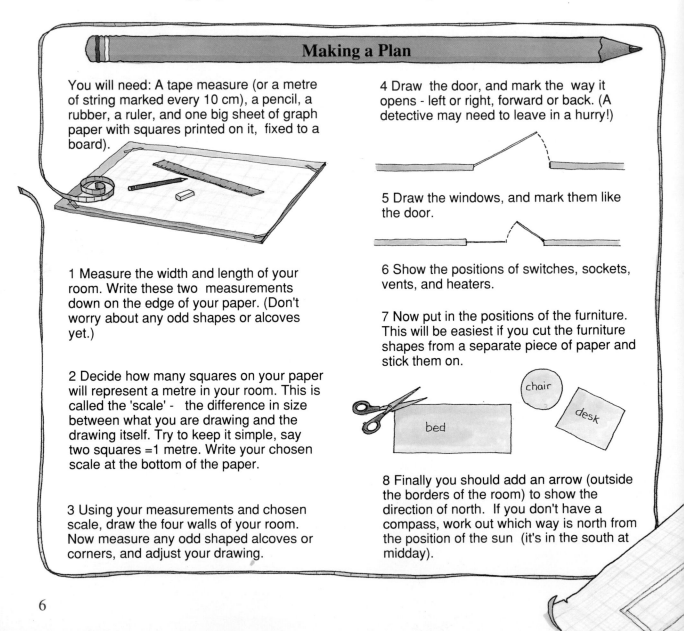

You will need: A tape measure (or a metre of string marked every 10 cm), a pencil, a rubber, a ruler, and one big sheet of graph paper with squares printed on it, fixed to a board).

1 Measure the width and length of your room. Write these two measurements down on the edge of your paper. (Don't worry about any odd shapes or alcoves yet.)

2 Decide how many squares on your paper will represent a metre in your room. This is called the 'scale' - the difference in size between what you are drawing and the drawing itself. Try to keep it simple, say two squares =1 metre. Write your chosen scale at the bottom of the paper.

3 Using your measurements and chosen scale, draw the four walls of your room. Now measure any odd shaped alcoves or corners, and adjust your drawing.

4 Draw the door, and mark the way it opens - left or right, forward or back. (A detective may need to leave in a hurry!)

5 Draw the windows, and mark them like the door.

6 Show the positions of switches, sockets, vents, and heaters.

7 Now put in the positions of the furniture. This will be easiest if you cut the furniture shapes from a separate piece of paper and stick them on.

chair

bed

desk

8 Finally you should add an arrow (outside the borders of the room) to show the direction of north. If you don't have a compass, work out which way is north from the position of the sun (it's in the south at midday).

HANDY HINT

Measure your 'handspan', the distance between your little finger and thumb at their widest stretch. This can be useful when you don't have a ruler. Also measure your foot, and your stride.

A Machine For Living In

Stand on the pavement outside your home and look at the ground. Your first clue has a small iron cover on it. This is the lid to a small metal box. Inside is a tap which controls the water supply coming into your house.

There will also be a (much larger) cover to the drain which carries dirty water away from your home. You will probably find other mysterious covers. These might be for telephone cables, gas pipes, cable TV or a fire hydrant. If you live in an old house with a cellar there might be a coal delivery hole. You can see a cover to one of these amongst the pictures below. See if you can detect what is underneath the other covers.

Not all essential services (power, water, telephones etc) enter the building under the ground. Stand outside and look up. Can you see telephone or electricity cables? Some homes have cable television. Can you see television aerials on your home?

The inside of your home is a machine for living in. All the services make it safe and comfortable. Can you imagine what it would be like to live in a home with no running water, heating, lights, electricity, telephones, or television? Not so long ago, homes had none of these things!

Find out how your home is heated. There are lots of different methods. How many weeks' pocket money do you think it would take to pay a month's heating bill? What sort of power is used for cooking in your home? Often it will be a mixture of gas and electricity.

electricity
sewer
water mains
gas mains

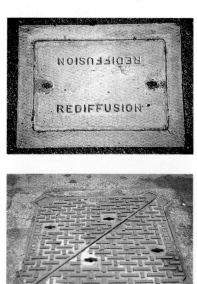

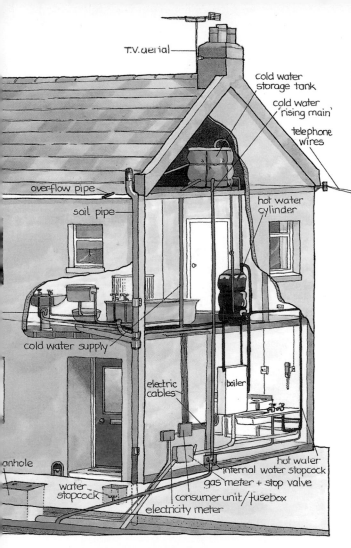

T.V. aerial

cold water storage tank

cold water 'rising main'

telephone wires

overflow pipe

soil pipe

hot water cylinder

cold water supply

electric cables

boiler

manhole

water stopcock

hot water

internal water stopcock

gas meter + stop valve

consumer unit/fusebox

electricity meter

FASCINATING FACTS:

Lavatory pans are designed with a bend called a trap. This holds enough water to prevent smells rising up the pipe from the main drain into the home.

The first power station was built in 1880 at Godalming in Surrey, to provide electricity for street lighting and private homes.

Making Rubbings

On a dry day, make a rubbing of every cover on the pavement outside your home. *Never make a rubbing in the road!*

You will need: A sheet of paper larger than the cover, a soft brush, a wax crayon, and some tape.

1 Brush off any loose grit from the cover.

2 Place your paper over the cover and tape down the edges.

3 Rub evenly over the paper with the whole side of the crayon.

4 Write on the paper the identity of the cover and its exact position.

Inside Information

Imagine you are a prisoner in your own home. You have to send information to a team of rescuers who have never been in the building. They will rescue you from your bedroom in the middle of the night! You have pencils and paper, but you can't speak to your team on the phone.

First, you will need to make a detailed plan of the building. It will be more complicated than the plan of your den, but the same principles apply. See page 6.

Remember that all the rooms must fit together. If your home is on more than one floor, you will need to draw separate plans for each.

Mark in all the doors and windows, and show which way they open. Note the sorts of locks.

Show any cupboards or other hiding places which might come in handy.

Note the kind of floor coverings in each room. Are the floors solid, or are there wooden floorboards? If any floorboards creak, mark them on your plan. Your rescuers will need to know where they can creep without being heard.

Above all, remember to show any stairs and mark the ones that squeak!

Write in each room what it is used for, who uses it most, and at what times of the day.

Write on your plan the address and date.

Now keep it somewhere safe. It could be incredibly useful to a fireman if there was ever a fire, and your home was full of smoke. But it could also be very useful to a burglar!

Past Evidence

Houses can change a great deal over the years. Walls are put up or removed, windows and doors moved, rooms or a garage may be added. Can you spot any evidence of alterations in your home? See if you can find any plans of your home before your family moved in to it.

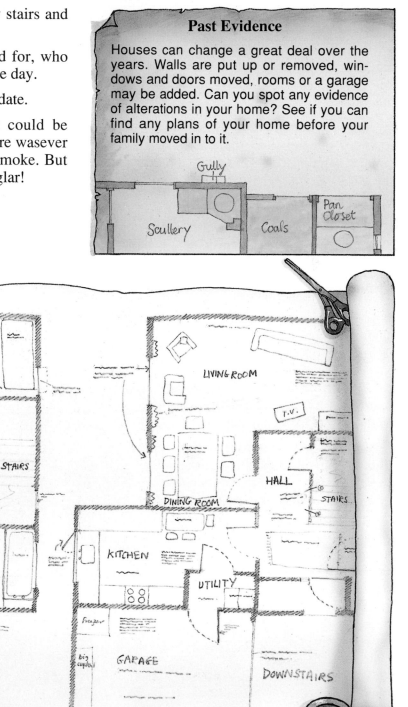

The Plot

No, this plot is not a secret plan. But you can still use all your skills as a detective to find out about it.

Another meaning of 'plot' is a piece of land - in this case the land on which your home stands. What makes your plot different from the others around it? How would you describe it to your rescuers?

Once all the land was open countryside. Have you ever wondered when and why it was divided up into the plots which you see now? This could be a fascinating case for an urban detective to investigate.

Start by visiting your local reference library. There should be some old maps of your area which can tell you all sorts of things. The librarian will show you local history books too. For more clues and tips about maps and historical investigations, there are other books in the Urban Detective series.

Sometimes houses, gardens and streets fit into the pattern of old field systems. Or there may have been a large house that was demolished and the land divided up and built on again. The name of your street may give a clue to the previous use of the land. For example: 'Foundry Street' may have been the site of a foundry. If the name of the street includes the name 'gardens' it may once have been a market garden.

flowerbed

rotary clothes drier

Pond

shed

tree

patio

tree

grass

wooden fence 1.5m high

Back Door

gravel path

MY HOUSE

① dustbin

1.3m high

side entrance

Brick wall

pebbles

concrete

Old house on 4 floors
Now 6 flats

garage

front door

№13

crazy paving

Noggle

flowers

low fence

apple tree

dustbins

№15

1990's

Parking area (tarmac)

(1870's)

№15

BLES

A Plan of the Plot

Draw a plan showing the shape of your plot, and how it fits into its neighbours on all sides and on to the road. Try to get the shapes of all the plots right and make them fit into each other. Show what marks the boundaries. You will probably get a better view from an upstairs window.

Outline the ground covered by the building you live in.

Mark the entrances to the plot.

What is on the ground? Outline paths and label different areas.

Are there any trees to hide behind or climb for a better view? Is there a shed, greenhouse, pond, swing or sand pit? Where is the dustbin kept? Mark these on the plan. Your rescuers would not want to fall over things in the dark!

At Home with Nature

x3

Are you ever alone in your home? There are other people around most of the time, and perhaps you have some pets. But is that all?

There are thousands of creatures sharing your living space! Quite a miniature zoo, in fact. Many are far too small to see. Others may need some detective work to find. Most leave clues to their presence.

Here are some of the animals you might see if you look carefully.

Houseflies : very common insects in our homes. They eat any food left uncovered, and can spread germs.
Clue - Look and listen. Dead flies are often found in light fittings and by windows. What do you think killed them?

Bugs and Beetles: Some bugs and beetles like to live indoors. In nature, many like eating dead trees. There are a lot of these in most homes - think about it.

House Spider: This creature lives in most homes. It eats harmful insects, but can't hurt you, and is much more frightened of you than you may be of it. During the night it goes 'walkabout' and sometimes is unlucky enough to fall into the bath, where someone finds it in the morning.

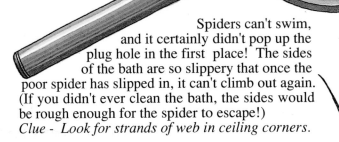

x2

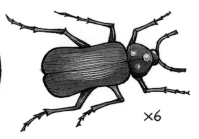

x6

Spiders can't swim, and it certainly didn't pop up the plug hole in the first place! The sides of the bath are so slippery that once the poor spider has slipped in, it can't climb out again. (If you didn't ever clean the bath, the sides would be rough enough for the spider to escape!)
Clue - Look for strands of web in ceiling corners.

Furniture Beetle: This beetle is also called woodworm. It lays its eggs on wood. When its larvae hatch they start to bore tunnels, chomping steadily. They can do a lot of damage.
Clue - Look for tiny holes in wood. These are where the adult beetles have emerged.

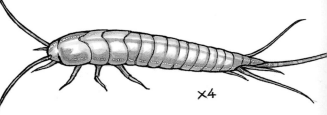

x4

x10

Mites: You might never see a mite, but even in the cleanest of homes there are hundreds of thousands of these microscopic creatures. Much of the dust in your home is food for one sort of mite or another.
Clue - Some people have an allergic reaction caused by dust mites.

Silverfish: Find somewhere dark and damp such as an undersink cupboard. It is likely that a silverfish will have found it too. It moves very fast, and mostly eats starchy crumbs.
Clue - Turn on the light suddenly at night and look for a flash of silvery scales.

14

Bed-Bugs: These creatures once shared most people's beds. Now we keep ourselves and our bedding cleaner they are quite rare, but you can even find them in new beds.
Clue - Little bites in the night!

Clothes Moths: They lay their eggs on fabrics. The larvae feed on spots of dirt and natural fibres. Nowadays people wash their clothes frequently in washing machines, so clothes moths are not very common any more.
Clue - Holes in clothes and household fabrics.

Wasps: Wasps are common in the summer months. They are attracted to sweet food and dustbins. They have a painful sting. Often they build nests in roof spaces, which can look surprisingly delicate and pretty.
Clue - If you see wasps buzzing around a roof there is probably a nest inside.

Bats: Bats like to inhabit house roofs, but are getting quite rare. You would be extremely lucky to have a bat sharing your home, and it would be protected by law. Most bats are very tiny and quiet. They will not hurt you.
Clue - Listen very carefully and watch the outside of your home at dusk.

Fleas: Pets always seem to catch fleas. These tiny insects live among their fur and suck their blood. They breed in pets' bedding. Sometimes they bite humans, but they don't like the flavour!
Clues - Pets scratching themselves a lot. Little specks like salt and pepper (eggs and droppings) on your pets' bedding.

House Mice: Pet mice are delightful, but mice living wild in the home can be a real nuisance. They run around at night, nibbling at food and almost anything else, including electric cables. They spread disease.
Clue - They leave droppings, and can sometimes be heard under floorboards, where they nest.

Background Information

How much do you know about your neighbours - the people you see almost every day of your life? Do you know their names, and what they do? Would you recognise them in another place? How different are they to your own family. And what about the buildings they live in? Are they the same as yours?

Perhaps you think you know the answers already, but a good detective can always discover more. Make it your aim to find out or notice one new thing about your street every day.

Neighbourhood Watch

Police like people to keep a close watch on their homes and help prevent crime by reporting anything suspicious. Of course, if you see anyone committing a crime, you should report it. But first of all it is a good idea to watch normal life on your street. Compile a logbook of what happens regularly. Who calls on which days, and at what time? Does the postman come more than once a day? Who delivers the newspapers? Is there a local window cleaner? Which other people visit your own home, and do they always come at the same times?

By making an information chart you will soon learn a lot more about your surroundings. At the top of the page, put the name of the street. Then take a building at a time, starting with your own, and list the things you know about it and the people who live or work in it.

You don't have to use the same headings. A clever detective will be able to think up others. You could end up filling a small notebook, rather than just having a chart.

While you are finding out about the street as it is now see what you can uncover about any changes made since the buildings were put up. Someone may have turned his front garden into a parking place. Or perhaps a shop has been converted into a house (clues such as old signs and large display windows). You might find extensions, double glazing, or rooms built into the roof.

PARK STREET

house number or name	type of building	use of building	names and number of occupants	occup
45	semi-detached	family home	John Brown Dav Brown Chris Leah	teache engine at school
47	semi-detached	home	Mrs Weaver (age 87)	old lady
49	single storey workshop	garage (car mechanic)	no one lives there. 4 workers	car mecha
43	detached	family home	Mr Sutton Mrs Sutton Janna (5) Robin (2)	salesman housewife
41	semi-			

Home Help!

'HELP!' A waterpipe in your home has just burst. Do you know what to do? An urban detective should always be prepared.

Of course you already know where to find the main water stopcock outside your home. You have made a rubbing of its cover. Lever the cover up with an old screwdriver until you can get your fingers beneath to lift it clear.

Which way does the tap turn? Most turn clockwise to shut *off*.

Once you have turned the mains water off, you should turn all the cold taps *on*. This lets most of the water out of the system into the drains, rather than all over your home through the leak.

There may be other mains stopcocks inside your home. Find out where they are. See if you can detect where the water goes once it is inside your home. Normally it rises up a pipe (the rising main) to the attic, and is stored in a cold water tank. Then it goes down to the sinks, bath, shower, toilet, boiler, etc. The kitchen cold tap (drinking water) normally comes straight from the rising main.

Start to compile a 'Home Help list' for all the services like gas, electricity, water, and oil for central heating. There may be people in your home who don't know where stopcocks are located. A clear plan could even save lives!

Add more details to the home plan that you have already drawn. Start by marking the positions of inside water taps, then all the power points and light switches.

Ask an adult to show you where the fuse box or consumer unit and electricity meter are. Mark them on your plan. There will be one (usually larger) switch, which is the main on/off control.

Warning: Electricity used carelessly can kill you. It is particularly lethal when combined with water. NEVER fiddle with plugs, fuses or switches unless there is a competent adult with you.

Plugged In!

Learn to wire up a plug and put in the correct fuse.

Make sure that an adult supervises and checks what you are doing. It is very fiddly, and most adults hate the job. You may be in great demand if you become good at it.

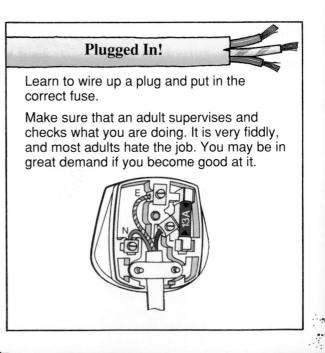

Do you know what gas smells like? The natural gas in our homes doesn't have a strong smell, so the gas board add strong-smelling chemicals to help identify it .

Gas escapes can be very dangerous and cause explosions. If you have a gas leak, you should turn off the mains gas supply, which will be a lever beside the meter. (Mark this on your plan too). Open windows and call the gas board. Leave the house, and do not operate *any* electrical switches, or light naked flames.

The telephone is useful for summoning help, so you should know how to use it. Practise looking things up in the telephone directories and Yellow Pages. Perhaps you have more than one telephone in your home? Mark the positions of any 'phones or 'phone sockets on your plan.

Do you know anyone with an answerphone? These can be very useful, as you can leave messages for people who aren't in. Practise talking to one. It feels strange at first. You must be able to leave a clear, short message.

If you need the police, ambulance, or fire engine urgently, dial 999. Remain calm, and be ready to give clear information.

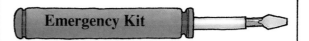

Emergency Kit

Assemble a basic emergency kit. It could contain a torch and spare battery, household cartridge fuses of different ratings, spare plug, scissors, fusewire, an insulated or electrical screwdriver, an ordinary and a Philips screwdriver, a Stanley knife, string, Sellotape, notepaper, insulated pliers, and a hammer.

Add a list of emergency telephone numbers: gas board, electricity board, police, family doctor, plumber, nearest relatives, and anyone else who might be useful in an emergency at home.

Just Around the Corner

Now it's time to get out and about. How well do you think you know your own neighbourhood - the streets you travel along to get to school, the local shops and open spaces? Are you really observant about everyday things, or do you just see what you expect?

Here are two challenges:

1 Pretend you are walking past your nearest row of shops. Make a list, from memory, of their names and what they sell. Write the list in the order that you would walk past them. Now do the same journey for real. How accurate is your memory?

2 Make a photocopy or tracing of your part of town from a street map. Draw a circle round your home about 800 metres across. Then take a pair of scissors, and remove this section. Tape a piece of blank paper behind the hole and, without looking at the missing piece of map, redraw your neighbourhood area from memory. Mark in the street names, railway lines, parks etc. Then compare your memory map with the real map. How did you do?

Mystery Tour

This game can take you on lots of new routes through your local area. Play it with a friend and have fun.

Make some cards about the size of playing cards. You could start by photocopying the examples below and cutting them out. On each card, write a clue and draw a picture.

Shuffle the cards. Then walk along the streets with the cards until you have seen or done the thing that is written on each card, in order.

Find a piece of litter and put it in a bin.

Look for a cat.

You need to post a letter. Find a Pillar-Box.

Take the next right turn.

Find a seat.

Sit down for two minutes.

AY·F 31·BE

A3·15 T·DP

Find two car number plates starting with A

Peep through a crack in a fence.

Find some stained glass

Collect 3 different leaves.

Walk past six yellow things.

Telephone

Go to a telephone box.

By shuffling the cards, and adding new ones of your own, you can create many mystery tours.

RULES: Tell an adult what you are going to do, and roughly where you will be. Be Streetwise (see page 2). Keep out of private gardens, and be careful crossing roads.

Presenting the Evidence

A criminal detective must first solve the crime. Then comes the difficult bit... presenting a convincing report. Facts must be accurate, notes in order, deductions clearly reasoned, and evidence neatly displayed.

An urban detective has much the same job. What are you going to do with the information you collect? Storage methods range from computers to old envelopes - the most important thing is to be well organized.

You have probably started to collect pieces of paper that are all different sizes and shapes, maybe also booklets and objects.

A Card Index

This a smaller version of the box file, normally organized with dividers for each letter of the alphabet. It holds postcard-sized cards for writing your notes on. You can buy or make one.

A Ring Binder

This has the advantage that once you have sorted your information, it will stay in order. You can also insert labelled subject dividers.

It can be made attractive to look at, and is a good way to present a project for school. If you are including photographs and maps, etc, mount them first on to paper or thin card of the size that the binder takes.

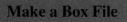

Make a Box File

You can buy box files in stationers, but they're expensive. If you make them yourself you can choose the size and shape.

Find an empty cardboard box of a suitable size.

To make the box more attractive, cover it with left-over wallpaper, wrapping paper, or pictures from colour supplements.

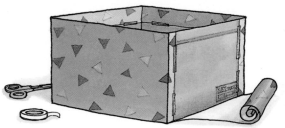

Cut pieces of card to fit inside it, as subject dividers. Decide for yourself how many dividers you need.

Cut tabs as shown, for labelling.

Label the dividers, and store your findings in the system.

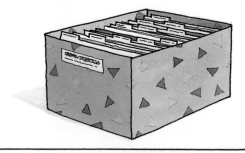

An Exhibition

Why not mount an exhibition? Arrange the material on big sheets of card before you stick it down.

Label everything as clearly as you can. Important information, such as the title of the exhibition, should be in bigger letters. If you don't want to write straight on to the big sheets, stick labels on afterwards.

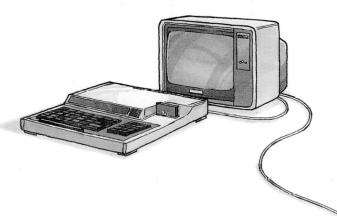

Detective's Database

Do you have access to a computer? If so, you can be very up to date, and store your information on discs or tapes. Don't forget to make back-up copies and print out hard copy (on paper) if you can.

A Photograph Album

If you have a camera, add your own photographs to the collection of evidence. Find some picture postcards of your local area. You may even find some family photographs of your house and town.

If you can't afford to buy an album, a cheap scrapbook can be made to look just as good. Always label your photos with the place and date.

Spoken Evidence

If you make recordings on interviews, always label the tape and its box. You can also write down the information, and use the tape again.

Tips for presenting evidence

Always try to be neat, tidy, and organised.

Label things clearly.

Title your project, and don't forget to put your name and the date on it.

Try to write a brief introduction about your collection and work.

If it is a school project, deliver it on time. Try to think of a different way to present your work, if everyone in the class is doing the same thing.

Your own Model Town

By making your own cardboard models you can create a street, neighbourhood, or even a whole town.

Each book in this series gives different ideas and has new model templates for you to adapt. You can of course design your own templates.

Most buildings are fairly simple shapes, so it can be quite straight forward to make tiny model versions.

The easiest way to start is to use these templates. They must not be cut out of the book, but may be photocopied and coloured.

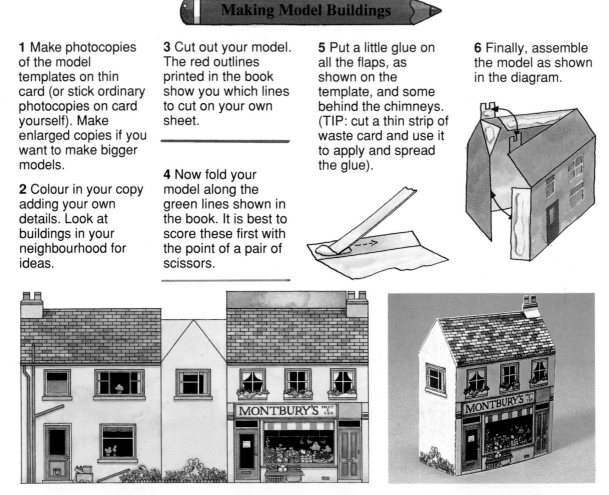

Making Model Buildings

1 Make photocopies of the model templates on thin card (or stick ordinary photocopies on card yourself). Make enlarged copies if you want to make bigger models.

2 Colour in your copy adding your own details. Look at buildings in your neighbourhood for ideas.

3 Cut out your model. The red outlines printed in the book show you which lines to cut on your own sheet.

4 Now fold your model along the green lines shown in the book. It is best to score these first with the point of a pair of scissors.

5 Put a little glue on all the flaps, as shown on the template, and some behind the chimneys. (TIP: cut a thin strip of waste card and use it to apply and spread the glue).

6 Finally, assemble the model as shown in the diagram.

An example of how you can colour your own model shop.

The finished model

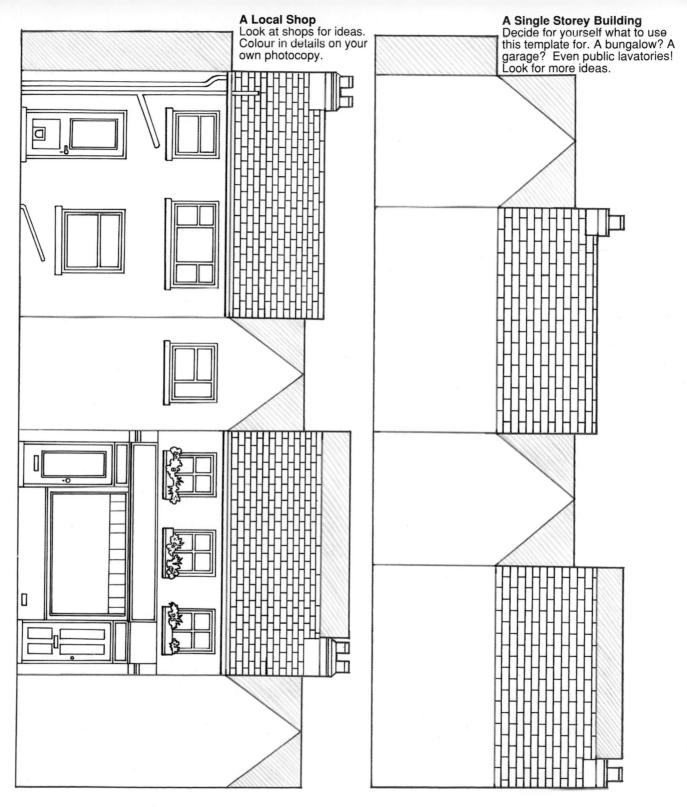

A Local Shop
Look at shops for ideas.
Colour in details on your
own photocopy.

A Single Storey Building
Decide for yourself what to use
this template for. A bungalow? A
garage? Even public lavatories!
Look for more ideas.

Books to Read

Wigwams, Igloos & Bungalows, Elizabeth Hogarth (Piccolo/Pan 1977)
The Living Town, Michael Pollard (Holt, Rinehart & Winston 1985)
The Environment, Peter Campbell et al (Oliver & Boyd 1985)
The Wildlife in Your Home, Terry Jennings (Young Library 1984)
Micro-Life in Rubbish, Morgens Jansen (Longman 1981)
History Around You : Starter Book, Dorothy Morrison (Oliver & Boyd 1983)
History Around You : Book 4, L E Snellgrove (Oliver & Boyd 1983)
Investigating Homes, C B Green (Arnold-Wheaton 1985)
Building a House, J G Raitt (Macdonald 1979)
Towns and Town Life, Alan Hammersley (Blandford Press 1969)
Parks and Gardens, Michael Chinery (Kingfisher Books 1985)
All About Your Street, Stephen Scoffam (Cambridge University Press 1983)
The Local Environment, Richard Kemp (Macdonald 1984)
The Urban Scene, Philip Neal (Dryad Press Ltd 1987)
Outset Geography, Simon Catling, Tim Firth & David Rowbottam (Oliver & Boyd 1981)
Local Issues, Robert Stephenson (Nelson 1989)
Seen Locally, Henry Pluckrose (Routledge 1989)

Acknowledgements

Photographs Bob Seago: 24, cover. The remaining photographs: Jane Launchbury and Lewis Cohen Urban Studies Centre at Brighton Polytechnic.
Artwork Seeboard 18 (plug diagram). All other artwork: Jane Launchbury.
Research Assistance Denise Francis.

Selma Montford is the director of the Lewis Cohen Urban Studies Centre based at Brighton Polytechnic. It is an information and resource centre concerned with understanding the local environment.

There may be an Urban Studies Centre in your area; for a list of all Urban Studies Centres contact: the National Association for Urban Studies, Canterbury USC, 82 Alphege Lane, Canterbury, Kent CT1 2EB

Index

A number in **bold** type means there is a picture